ALL TIME HEROES
FROM ALL TIMES

~ Volume 6 ~

SAINT SHENOUDA PRESS

All Time Heroes

from All Times

~ Volume 6 ~

The Life of St Mary
The Mother of God

ST SHENOUDA'S MONASTERY
SYDNEY, AUSTRALIA
2020

All Time Heroes From All Times - Volume 6
THE LIFE OF ST MARY THE MOTHER OF GOD

ST SHENOUDA PRESS
8419 Putty Rd,
Putty, NSW, 2330
Australia

www.stshenoudapress.com
ISBN 13: 978-0-9945710-3-8

Translator: Nadia Farag

Cover Design:
Hani Ghaly,
Begoury Graphics
begourygraphics@gmail.com

CONTENTS

THE BIRTH OF ST. MARY

ST. MARY, THE WOMAN OF PRAYER AND PROMISED DAUGHTER FROM THE WOMB

St. Mary's father Joachim was a shepherd of goats just like his previous forefathers Abraham, Isaac and Jacob. He lived in Jerusalem and longed for someone to shepherd his goats in the mountains. St. Mary's mother was named Hannah, after one of Aaron's daughters. Both of St. Mary's parents were descendants from the tribe of Judah, the house of David. Both were righteous in the eyes of Lord and followed His word and commandments. They praised the Lord day and night, fervently asking Him to grant them a child. The Lord heard their prayers and answered their request.

The Lord was so pleased with St. Mary that He chose her from birth to carry His son who cannot be contained either by heaven or earth. God sent His angel to her parents to announce the birth of the Virgin St. Mary. The Lord knew her even before she was formed. He blessed St. Mary in her mother's womb and filled her with the Holy Spirit. Thus, St. Mary was called by God to be a woman of prayer when God sanctified and blessed her in the womb.

St. Mary was raised by her parents in the fear of the Lord in her early upbringing. As St. Mary was the blessed fruit of prayers promised by the Lord to her parents Joachim and Hannah, they lived as true children of God teaching St. Mary all about the wonderful works and the love of the Lord through their example.

ST. MARY IN THE TEMPLE OF SOLOMON

When St. Mary was one year old during the time of Zechariah as the high priest, it was said that the angel of the Lord asked Zechariah to remind her parents about their promise to dedicate St. Mary to serve the Lord in the temple. When St. Mary was three years old and could stand up by herself, she knew about the Lord from her parents which was foundational to her future growth. St. Mary entered the temple when she was only three years old and did not cry when her parents left her alone in the Lord's house. She was very quiet and meek, which amazed both the priests and Levites.

St. Mary's parents used to visit hear in the temple from time to time until her father passed away. St. Mary did not cry or was upset when her father departed but instead she was truly comforted by the words of her father David: "When my father and my mother forsake me, then the Lord will take care of me" (Ps 27:10) and from the prophecy about her: "Can a woman forget her nursing child, and not have compassion on the son of her womb? Surely they may forget, yet I will not forget you. See, I have inscribed you on the palms of my hands" (Is 49:15-16). Built upon this faith, St. Mary devoted her whole life to the Lord.

St. Mary felt that staying in the temple really is experiencing God's presence as the Lord blessed and sanctified the temple. St. Mary felt that she had to be pure in God's presence by reading holy books, praying, fasting and living according to the commandments of God and teachings of the elders.

In the temple, St. Mary, along with her companions,

learned God's commandments. Zechariah, the High Priest, cared for St. Mary where she grew physically and spiritually through obedience, love and complete devotion to Yahweh, the God of Israel. St. Mary truly felt that the temple was like heaven where God was sitting on His throne and she was sitting under His feet, attentively listening to His words and commandments.

FROM THE TEMPLE TO THE HOUSE OF ST. JOSEPH THE CARPENTER

St. Mary stayed in the temple until she was almost 11 years old. She learned many teachings and worshipped day and night through fasting, prayers and supplications. St. Mary surpassed all in memorising and applying the Word of God.

According to the Jewish teachings a girl could not stay in the temple after 14 years of age, thus St. Mary was forced to leave the temple. After leaving the temple St. Mary needed to be taken care of by a responsible guardian. According to the Jewish customs and practices, twelve elders were selected to decide who would be chosen to care for St. Mary. Each of the twelve elders had their wooden rods marked with their names and their rods were placed in the temple. A fasting period then followed and at the end of the fasting period, a dove would land on one of the rods. The owner of that rod would be selected as the guardian. At the conclusion of the fasting period to decide who would care for St. Mary, St. Joseph the Carpenter was selected. Everyone who was present in the temple trusted that God selected St. Joseph to care for St. Mary. Thus, the Virgin St. Mary left the temple for St. Joseph's house in the city of Nazareth.

THE ANNUNCIATION OF ARCHANGEL GABRIEL TO ST. MARY

While St. Mary was under the care of St. Joseph and staying at his house in Nazareth, she constantly recited and meditated on the word of God day and night, and was especially touched with the prophetic words about the coming Messiah. When the Lord found such righteous qualities in St. Mary, He announced that she would bear Christ incarnate in the flesh and filled her with the Holy Spirit.

The archangel Gabriel came to St. Mary when he proclaimed to her; peace for her fullness of God's grace, that the Lord was with her and that she was blessed among women.

Since the apparitions of angels were quite uncommon St. Mary was troubled by the angel's appearance. The angel comforted her by saying:

1- You have found favor in God's eyes more than any woman in the world

2- The Lord proclaims that you will conceive and bring forth a Son and that you shall call His name Jesus

3- That He will be great and will be called the Son of the Highest

4- That the Lord God will give Him the throne of His father David

5- That He will reign over the house of Jacob forever

6- That His kingdom will have no end

When St. Mary's fear vanished and was comforted that God was with her, she told the angel that she was only engaged to St. Joseph for protection and care. Logically since St. Mary was a virgin who had never known a man, she questioned how she could conceive a son?

The angel explained that:

1- The Holy Spirit will come upon her

2- The power of the Highest will overshadow her

3- The child Jesus will be called the Son of God

4- With God nothing will be impossible

The angel also told St. Mary that Elizabeth, who was barren, had conceived a son of six months despite her old age.

After these proclamations, St. Mary accepted and submitted to the Lord saying: "Behold the maidservant of the Lord. Let it be to me according to your word" (Luke 1:38)

ST MARY'S JOURNEY FROM NAZARETH
TO THE CITY OF JUDAH

Through the Holy Spirit St. Mary conceived Jesus in her womb and when she knew that Elizabeth was pregnant in her old age she was overflowing with joy. St. Mary took permission from her husband to visit her relative and rose early in the morning into the mountains, the city of Judah. St. Mary was not too concerned about the dangers of the mountainous road since she felt a strong confidence that God was with her. Throughout the journey St. Mary was reciting what the angel of God had told her: "the things which are impossible with men are possible with God" (Lk 18:27).

St. Mary was wondering in her heart whether there was a connection between the announcement that Angel Gabriel declared to Zachariah about his son's birth and the annunciation that she would conceive and give birth to the Son of God. St. Mary felt confident that God brought about a connection between the birth of Elizabeth's son in Judah and the birth of her child, even though St. Mary was unsure exactly where He would be born.

St. Mary then remembered what she had been taught in the temple when Isaiah the prophet wrote about a child being born before the Messiah and what his work would be: "The voice of one crying in the wilderness: "Prepare the way of the Lord; make straight in the desert a highway for our God. Every valley shall be exalted and every mountain and hill brought low; the crooked places shall be made straight and the rough places smooth; the glory of the Lord shall be revealed, and all flesh shall see it together; for the mouth of the Lord has spoken" (Is 40:3-5).

ST. MARY IN BETHLEHEM

Bethlehem, which is a Jewish name meaning house of bread, is a small village located about six miles South of Jerusalem. At that time Bethlehem was surrounded by hills covered with trees and beautiful shrubs. Bethlehem also had fresh water springing underground of which King David, along with his father's herd used to drink from. This village was where Rachael, the beloved wife of our father Jacob, was buried (Gen 35:19). Bethlehem was also where Ruth, Nemaha and Boaz lived (Ruth 1:19-22) and where King David was born. Reference to its greatness is found in the holy annunciation: "But you, Bethlehem, in the land of Judah, are not the least among the rulers of Judah; for out of you shall come a ruler who will shepherd my people Israel." (Matt 2:6)

WHY DID ST. MARY GO TO BETHLEHEM?

As soon as St. Mary returned from visiting Elizabeth and settled in her house, Augustus Caesar decreed that a census be taken. Everyone had to travel to their own town to register for the census.

Conducting a census was considered a routine task to decree for Caesar, yet for St. Mary there was a great plan of God behind this simple decree that Caesar could not have not known about at the time. This request by Augustus Caesar that a census be taken fulfilled the divine inspiration that ways of God are far above man's ways. God, who knows the hearts of all and controls the universe had a set timing for the census according to His heavenly plan.

We wonder why Caesar ordered the census at that time, particularly after the angel's annunciation to St. Mary nine months previously? Caesar had no knowledge of what happened in the temple or Nazareth and made the decree solely to account for the number of people he was governing in the east and west. Caesar was only concerned about his power so that he would be able to appoint the right number of rulers to control his empire, rather than St. Mary who he had no real knowledge of at the time. By ordering the census, Caesar was unknowingly fulfilling God's will that was promised beforehand. This is evidence that 'the king's heart is in the hand of the Lord, like the rivers of water; He turns it wherever He wishes' (Proverbs 21:1).

St. Mary went with St. Joseph to register for the census in Bethlehem. This was at the same time when God prophesised "But you Bethlehem, in the land of Judah, are not the least among the rulers of Judah; for out of you shall come a ruler who will shepherd my people Israel" (Matt 2:6) and "And He will reign over the House of Jacob forever, and of His kingdom there will be no end" (Luke 1:33).

The journey to Bethlehem was difficult and tiring for St. Mary who was in the last trimester of her pregnancy. It was also quite cold in winter and raining heavily. When St. Mary and St. Joseph arrived at Bethlehem, they did not have a place to stay because the town was overcrowded by people coming to register for the census. God's love however, organised a place in a manger for St. Mary and St. Joseph at the right time when her hour of delivery had come.

Who would have thought that the manger would be the crown for the Holy Child? Truly this would have been a great liberation that the human mind would find incomprehensible.

The Lord of Lords became a man like us, except without sin. One can ask where were the angelic praises during this birth? Where were the Seraphim and Cherubim with the six wings? Where were all the heavenly myriad of angels? Did they all cease their praising? All of them were present around the manger where the Son, the Word of God was born. The manger became a sanctified place where God was incarnate of a Virgin.

Who could have revealed this heavenly mystery with a pure heart? Only one with a heart full of grace, truth and faith. Both St. Mary and St. Joseph had pure hearts that God allowed to accept the coming of God incarnate. They were waiting day and night for the arrival of God incarnate, who would change the old human nature into a new one that would produce virtue and goodness.

THE MANGER IN BETHLEHEM

When we contemplate on the manger of Bethlehem, the following becomes evident:

1. Humility in its furthest extent is giving and sacrificing oneself.

When Christ was due to be born there was no available place for Him to stay; the only place available was in an animal manger. Choosing this place for His birth confuses the human mind as it brings forth the question of why He would accept to be born in this humble place? Christ answered that since He is the Son of God, He came to teach man to reject the vanities of this world that would lead man into sin and lack of faith. Christ wanted man to return to the Lord in mercy and forgiveness, and that He can find peace and safety by satisfying the merciful judge who does not want the death of a sinner. Christ wants all people to repent and receive forgiveness through the incarnate Son of God, who was born of the Virgin St. Mary.

The manger in Bethlehem carries many symbolisms revealed through divine inspiration. When Eve was in paradise, she longed to be like God; she disobeyed the word of God, fell into sin and was kicked out of paradise. Eve deserved the sentence of death just like her children, and had no choice but to accept her discipline. However, God desired to remove this sentence of death through the incarnate Son of God, born of the Virgin St. Mary. When St. Mary was born the heavens were overjoyed and made the annunciation, through the archangel Gabriel, that she would bring forth the Son of God. Initially St. Mary was overwhelmed with astonishment about how she could have a child without knowing a man? God spoke to her through the angel Gabriel by answering that the Holy Spirit would fill her. St. Mary believed in the prophecy of God and said that she was His servant. The heavenly conception of St. Mary led her to greater humility and self-denial, making her worthy to be called the Second Eve; the mother of whom would crush the head of the serpent and restore us, with His grace, to our original state.

2. From Spiritual Growth into the Fullness of Christ

From one perspective a manger was characteristic of changing from its original purpose, constantly changing with the world; one day it could be a manger, the following day it might change into a hut or dwelling, or even become a castle. From another perspective, in light of the spiritual saints, the world represented by the manger will disappear quickly, and not one stone shall be left here upon another, that shall not be thrown down. The believers in Christ are not conformed by the world and seek to live in the heavenly city, being saved by the grace of God. They do not have a continuing city in the world; they long for the everlasting one in the Bethlehem manger.

The land that flowing with milk and honey was defiled by sin when man fell. The land changed its nature and grew husks and thorns. According to the heavenly prophetic inspiration, the descendants of the woman will crush the head of the serpent (Gen 3:15). Thus, Christ being born in a humble manger allowed His grace to fill the earth.

The birth of Christ in the manger symbolised change; the change that the human mind could not have possibly imagined. The birth of Christ demonstrated that one should look at the heart of man, rather than the outside appearance. Being born in a humble manger might not have been acceptable for any human being, yet it was accepted by Jesus Christ. St. Paul described Christ; "who being in the form of God, did not consider it robbery to be equal with God, but made Himself of no reputation, taking the form of a bond servant, and coming in the likeness of men" (Philippians 2:6 -7).

The birth of Christ in a humble manger exemplified humility and silenced the mind of man who became in awe of God's wisdom. Subsequently one can now say, 'oh Lord your wisdom is exceedingly great and how unexplainable are your ways'. You blessed and sanctified the manger and adorned it with beauty, holiness and glory.

The manger has become a popular destination to visit by many people; emperors, kings and people from various nations continue to make pilgrimage and gain a blessing by visiting the exact place where Christ was born.

The birth of Christ proved the following:

1- The location itself does not honour the person, but rather it is the person who honors the place.

2-   The guidelines laid down by God are wiser than those laid down and governed by men driven by their own emotions and thoughts. Those who follow the commandments of God are protected and safe, in comparison to men who follow their own rules which are driven by human emotions or thoughts.

• Who would have expected and imagined that somebody born in an animal barn in Bethlehem would have had highly ranked people and princes, such as the wise men, come and offer gifts of worship to a baby? The wisemen believed that their salvation would be founded in Christ as they witnessed that God humbled himself to be incarnate in the form of a man and be born in a manger.

• Who would have thought that Messiah would be

from the Jews - who Moses and the prophets had written about and the Jewish people had envisaged the Messiah as a great leader to sit on David's throne - would be born in a manger? Furthermore, who would have imagined that some Jewish shepherds, known as the wisemen, would have joyfully visited and worshipped the baby Jesus in a manger after being enlightened by the angels about His birth?

• Who would have thought that there would have been people who were afraid and anxious that the true savior and king would be born? In fact, Herod and His men killed 144000 infants in Bethlehem. These children were true martyrs who laid down the foundation of martyrdom after Christ's resurrection.

• Who would have expected that one of the children of Bethlehem, Nathanael, who his mother had hidden under a fig tree and was saved from being killed, would meet Christ after 30 years and become His disciple? Incredibly Jesus told Nathanael that He had seen him under the fig tree, and then Nathanael declared to Christ that truly He is the Son of God and King of Israel.

ST. MARY'S DEVOTION IN KEEPING THE LAW

CIRCUMCISING THE BABY JESUS

When the Virgin St. Mary resided in the temple, she praised the Lord day and night. She memorised all of the old testament, keeping it close to her heart so that she could become a role model through her obedience and practice of its teachings.

By the time St. Mary knew that she would give birth to Christ, the Savior of the world, she understood that He would be a Jewish role model without blemish in His behavior and obedience to the Jewish law.

When the child Jesus was only eight days old, St. Mary asked St. Joseph to take the child to Jerusalem to be circumcised. St. Joseph offered Christ to be circumcised publicly in the temple. The prayers of circumcision were performed and the child was circumcised, just as the angel prophesied to St. Mary. The worshippers had a small humble celebration for Christ's circumcision after which St. Joseph, St. Mary and the baby Jesus all returned to Bethlehem.

St. Mary thanked the Lord as her son became one of God's people, the nation of Israel. As a Jew Christ could now enter the temple, learn the law and have the right to teach the Jewish people who would later listen to Him as a teacher and leader. Since He was born under the law, He would save those under the law. On the day of His circumcision, He became known to all the nations that His work on earth would be to save mankind.

IN ST. MARY'S PURIFICATION

The Virgin St. Mary stayed in Bethlehem for forty days respecting and following the Jewish law. She did not go with St. Joseph when the child Jesus was circumcised. When St. Mary finished her days of purification she went with St.

Joseph and the child Jesus to offer up burnt and sin offerings; which were two doves in front of the tabernacle so that the priest would give their offerings.

After St. Mary's purification and offerings, both St. Joseph and St. Mary met with some people who, through the guidance of the Holy Spirit, prophesied about the salvation of Israel through Christ.

A- SIMEON THE ELDER

And behold, there was a man in Jerusalem whose name was Simeon, and this man was just and devout, waiting for the Consolation of Israel, and the Holy Spirit was upon him. And it had been revealed to him by the Holy Spirit that he would not see death before he had seen the Lord's Christ. So he came by the Spirit into the temple. And when the parents brought in the Child Jesus, to do for Him according to the custom of the law, he took Him up in his arms and blessed God and said: "Lord, now You are letting Your servant depart in peace, according to Your word; For my eyes have seen Your salvation which You have prepared before the face of all peoples, A light to bring revelation to the Gentiles, And the glory of Your people Israel." (Lk 2:28-32)

St. Joseph and St. Mary were amazed at what Simeon prophesied, while St. Mary kept all these things in her heart.

B- HANNAH, THE DAUGHTER OF PHANUEL

Hannah was a gracious woman from the tribe of Asher. She lived with her husband for seven years before becoming a widow. If we assume, she was married when she was 16 years old and became a widow when she was about 23 years old, she stayed in the temple for about 84 years.

Hannah worshipped the Lord with fasting, prayers and supplications day and night in a special place for widows and virgins in the temple. She was known and respected by all the visitors in the temple. Hannah became a prophetess and was telling those who were studying the word of God about her prophecy that the savior would be coming soon to Jerusalem.

Hannah, the prophetess, would have been about 107 years old when she met the Virgin St. Mary. When Hannah saw St. Mary with a baby in her womb, she proclaimed that the child was Jesus. She praised the Lord for saving humanity through the incarnation of Jesus Christ. Hannah joined Simeon the elder in praising the incarnate Lord.

Hannah's proclamation was considered great evidence

that Jesus was the Son of God. It also proved that the New Testament gave women the same equal rights to men as Hannah stood beside Simeon the elder in proclaiming the Savior of the world.

VIRGIN MARY AND EGYPT

DEPARTURE TO EGYPT

There were several reasons why St. Mary needed to depart from Bethlehem to Egypt.

•   The angel announced to St. Joseph the first reason for the departure to Egypt since Herod intends to find the child Jesus and kill Him (Matthew 2:13).

When the shepherds did not return to Herod after visiting the child Jesus in the manger, He was furious. Herod considered this disobedient act as making a mockery out of him and he showed his jealousy and hatred towards the Messiah, the King of the Jews, when he ordered the killing of all male children less than two years old. In this negative state Herod decided with his human way of thinking to kill Jesus before He had slipped from his hands and fled.

• The Lord's eyes never sleep and His continuous love and care for humanity did not allow evil to control God's children. In the silence of the night, while St. Joseph was asleep in Bethlehem, the angel of the Lord appeared to him in a dream and said: "Arise, take the young child and His mother, flee to Egypt, and stay there until I bring you word; for Herod will seek the young Child to destroy Him" (Matthew 2:13). St. Joseph obeyed immediately and got up, took the child and the Virgin St. Mary during the night and fled to Egypt.

• The second reason was not as clearly apparent. It was to fulfil the promise of the prophecies.

St. Joseph rose promptly at night, woke up St. Mary who took her child, and set them on his donkey to travel to Egypt. Without a doubt the angel was their guide and the prophecies were fulfilled; "Behold, the Lord rides on a swift cloud, and will come into Egypt" (Is 19:1) and, "when Israel was a child, I loved him, and out of Egypt I called my Son" (Hosea 11:1) and Isaiah also said, "whom the Lord of Hosts shall bless saying "blessed is Egypt my people" (Isaiah 19:25).

ON THE WAY TO EGYPT

Due to the short distance between the Palestinian and the Egyptian land, anyone who sought some rest or help, or even to flee from any injustice in Palestine, would head to Egypt. They could travel to the land of Egypt in about three days. The Arish valley, which was the low area of the valley, was known as the Egyptian valley and anyone could pass that valley safely.

When it was revealed to St. Joseph during night to take the child Jesus and the Virgin St. Mary to Egypt, he told St. Mary and both immediately obeyed. They left at night probably to avoid attention, taking only a few supplies. St. Mary sat on the donkey carrying Jesus, while St. Joseph walked beside them. They travelled without fear or worry since the angel assured St. Joseph that they were guided under God's protection.

As the new day dawned, the young family would have left the populated area and started their walk in the wilderness towards the Egyptian border. St. Mary, St. Joseph and the child Jesus were confident that a myriad of angels were protecting them. They reached the city of Fermat, part of El Arish which is now Port Fouad, on the 24th of Bashans. They camped outside for a night in Ferma and on the second day they continued their travel reaching Basta Hills – which is Zagazeeg today. This area was considered the beginning of the Egyptian border, and was part of the Eastern District.

IN THE LAND OF EGYPT

The Holy Family passed through several districts when travelling across Egypt. After crossing the Nile river into the midst of the delta they progressed to el Mennea, which is close to the town of Samanood. Then the Holy Family passed through Samanood to cross into the Western side of the Nile river before they reached the Burles and Mokatam Monastery. Then the Holy Family proceeded southwards towards El Natron valley and gained special blessings by this visit. After that the Holy Family progressed into inner Egypt through the Nile river. They also passed through El Bahnasaa close to Samaloot, El Ashmonien, Esna Meir, Boog town, El Tamasehia El Saragna and El Gooseia before settling down in Jabal El Gosgam where the El Meharag Monastery is currently present. At the El Meharag Monastery a historical church is built to commemorate that the Holy Family stayed in a particular cave there.

THE RETURN TO BETHLEHEM AND NAZARETH

When the angel of the Lord informed St. Joseph about the deaths of Herod and other people who were attempting to kill the child Jesus, the Holy Family decided to return to Palestine. They returned using the same path as their arrival. The return path of the Holy Family to Palestine included travelling from Gosgam wilderness to Manf (The Delta Point) through the Nile river into what is currently known as Masr El adeema (Old Egypt). It is in Old Egypt where the Holy Family spent some time in a cave where the Abi Sarga Church was established. Following this the Holy Family passed El Zeitoun district heading towards El Matareya, where currently situates the famous St. Mary tree where the family had rested under. A church in St. Mary's name was built there in 1925 A.D. The Holy Family rested there for some time, bringing an abundant blessing to the area. Shortly after the Holy Family travelled to what is currently known as St. Mary's Church in Mustard and continued their trip towards the Northern-Eastern border, from which they eventually returned to Palestine.

St. Joseph always thought that his family would live in Bethlehem like his ancestors and would always have fond and blessed memories in relation to St. Mary's annunciation and the works of the shepherds and wiseman. However, when St.

Joseph found out that Argelious succeeded his father Herod on the throne, he became frightened and instead of going to live in Bethlehem he settled with his family in a quiet suburb in Nazareth. This fulfilled the prophecy that Jesus would be called Nazarene.

The traditional writings of the church record that the Holy Family lived in Egypt for about two years. Anba Theophelis, the 23rd Pope of Alexandria, said in one of his books that the Holy Family stayed in Egypt, away from Palestine, for precisely two years, three months and twenty-two days.

Although the Bible did not mention specifically what happened when the Holy Family came to Egypt, the traditional writings of the church record that when they passed Egyptian paganistic idols, or Greek or Roman temples, they all suddenly destroyed. Thus, the prophecy of Isaiah was fulfilled; "The burden against Egypt. Behold, the Lord rides on a swift cloud, and will come into Egypt; the idols of Egypt will totter at His presence, and the heart of Egypt will melt in its midst." (Is 19:1) The surprise must have been huge for the priests in these temples who would not have found any logical reason or cause for their destruction other than the passing of the humble Holy Family.

Egypt was blessed after the visit of the Holy Family. Undoubtedly the apparition of St. Mary in her church in Zeitoun in the 20th century was a confirmation also that God blessed Egypt saying: "Blessed are Egypt my people."

Whenever our faith wavers and is weakened through tribulations, the blessed St. Mary looks upon us through apparitions that strengthen and support us.

ST. MARY AT THE WEDDING OF CANA OF GALLILEE

THE APPEARANCES OF JESUS IN ISRAEL

In holy silence St. Mary had introduced her holy child to the non-believing world by the wiseman, and to the Jewish nation by the shepherds. Elizabeth's child was filled with the Holy Spirit after St. Mary visited her. All these people were honored by God and they worshipped Him through spirit and truth upon the moment of His annunciation and birth.

Before Jesus carried on His work as the redeemer of mankind, He lived as a man with physical attributes. Jesus prayed earnestly and fasted in order to be victorious when faced with many spiritual wars that were raised by the enemy of God.

Jesus chose His disciples and was their teacher, spiritual guide and role model. When Christ was invited to the wedding of Cana of Galilee, He took His disciples and mother also with Him. As St. Mary was in company of her Holy Son in the wedding, it would be appropriate for one to ask what St. Mary had heard from Jesus and kept in her heart to verify in due time and tell everyone about? She would have answered us calmly and humbly that the words she heard from heaven and kept in her heart are proof that God became incarnate of a virgin to redeem mankind from sin. It was God's will that everybody should be saved and come to God through His holy mysteries.

ST. MARY IN JESUS' EYE

Jesus confidently knew that His mother believed that God became incarnate. Jesus knew that He came on earth to do God's will; to help the weak, feel their agony and pain, and to have mercy on those tempted and in hardship.

Jesus knew that His mother had utmost belief and faith. Her peace was what helped her conquer the world and the enemy of goodness. Jesus knew that the devil was pursuing to constantly attack His mother. The devil might have left her for a brief time but would come back and try to harm her whenever she would proclaim the power of Jesus and demonstrate His strength in front of opposing leaders.

Jesus knew that St. Mary spoke about her son's glory in order for the world to know that Christ was sent by God the father, as the door to salvation. St. Mary proclaimed the name of Christ for the salvation of others rather than for her own self-exaltation or right as a mother. Jesus also knew that His mother had kept in her heart the words that He had said to her when He was twelve years old, saying "Why did you seek Me? Did you not know that I must be about My Father's business?" (Luke 2:49).

THE DIALOGUE AT THE WEDDING OF CANA OF GALILEE

"When they ran of wine, the mother of Jesus said to Him, "They have no wine". Jesus said to her: "Woman, what does your concern have to do with Me? My hour has not yet come." His mother said to the servants: "Whatever He says to you, do it" (Jn 2:3-5)… "Jesus said to them, "fill the waterpots with water." And they filled up to the brim. And He said to them, "Draw some out now, and take it to the master of the feast." (Jn 7-8). The master of the feast said that it was good wine. He asked the groom why he had kept the good wine until the end? When the groom questioned the source of the wine, he was told that it was water that Jesus converted into wine.

Jesus revealed His glory through the miracle of changing water into wine to His disciples and anybody else who was present. His disciples believed that He was God incarnated in the flesh. Many people who were present at the wedding of Cana of Galilee also believed that He was the coming Messiah to save the world.

THE SPIRITUAL MEANING OF THE WEDDING OF CANA OF GALILEE

To comprehend the true spiritual meaning of the dialogue that took place between St. Mary and her son Jesus Christ in the miracle at the wedding of Cana of Galilee, we have to listen carefully to what St. Mary said. We have to envisage that she remembered seeing Jesus baptized by John the Baptist and Christ choosing His disciples. St. Mary, arguably, believed that it was the fulfillment of time for Christ to come into the world so that all may believe in Him.

When St. Mary knew about the lack of wine at the wedding, she might have thought in her heart to go and tell Jesus about it, however, likely she then would have remembered His words when Christ said "I must be about My Father's business".

St. Mary would have comprehended Christ's intention to answer her. It appeared as if He was saying to her that He did not want anyone to hasten and announce Him to the world. Jesus wanted to reveal His glory to the Jews first and then to the gentiles. He wanted them to remember that God had mercy on them and had come for their salvation.

If we followed the dialogue closely, it might appear that Jesus was opposing St. Mary's words. However, this supposed opposition was clearly non-existent when St. Mary told them, "whatever He says to you, do it". St Mary knew that the hour had come for the Father to be glorified by the Son.

Those who opposed Christ seemed to disappear when Jesus asked that the waterpots be filled with water. With Christ's words He confirmed the great faith of St. Mary as her strong belief was accompanied by love.

When Jesus asked that the wine be offered to the master of the feast, the water was found to have changed into very good wine, just like St. Mary had wanted. This miracle clearly showed that St. Mary's will conferred with Jesus's will, and also showed the glory of Jesus to the Israelites. The conversion of water to wine was the first public miracle that Jesus had performed in front of His disciples. Many people believed in Jesus from that moment on and crowds started following Him.

The words of Christ to His mother would have reminded her of what Simeon said when he carried Jesus as a baby. Simeon said that a sword will pierce her heart when the salvation would be delivered. It appeared as if Christ was saying to His mother; "How can I, woman, cause you more pain and heartache due to your glorification for my miracles and good works? When you brought me forth into the world as God incarnated in the flesh and the coming Messiah into the world, you would have to bear tribulations and attacks from the enemy of mankind. However, do not be troubled and worried in hardship and attacks from Satan but be strong and encourage my brethren in faith that they conquer the enemy"

The conversion of water into wine was also a blessing and glorification of the name of Jesus. Christ performing the miracle demonstrated compassion and kindness to the people attending the wedding. He drove away the feeling of shame of not being able to meet their duty of being good hosts. Also, by attending the wedding too, Jesus had uplifted the morale and self-esteem of those present and blessed the physical place itself.

ST. MARY'S SUPPLICATION IN THE WEDDING

In many of our hymns in the church from the beginning of the liturgical prayers until the end, we ask St. Mary to supplicate before us in front of her son to forgive our sins. Whenever we lift our hearts to the Lord through the intercessions and prayers of St. Mary, we visualise ourselves in front of Christ and the supplications of His mother, who supplicated Jesus to change the water into wine.

St Mary's prayers and guidance towards to follow God's word is evidenced when she said to the servants, "whatever He says to you, do it". St. Mary wants us to obey God with complete submission and obedience so that we gain His goodness and glory.

St. Mary continually supplicates for the world. She asks her son to enrich us in our spiritual and physical lives. Christ listens to her because her supplications are to glorify her son in front of everybody and to have their sins forgiven as they glorify His Holy Name.

ST. MARY IN FRONT
OF THE CROSS

ST. MARY'S SUFFERING AND SWORDS
PIERCING HER SOUL

The word of God declares that the Queen will sit on the right hand of the King in heaven. When Christ came to Earth, He concentrated His teachings on repentance and seeking the kingdom of God. Christ demonstrated great mercy and compassion in His life on earth. He truly was a teacher and a spiritual doctor, healing the sick and raising the dead.

Many believers had ambitions of sitting next to Christ in heaven, as seen in the account of the   mother of Zebedee's sons; "Then the mother of Zebedee's sons came to Him with her sons, kneeling down and asking something from Him. And He said to her, "What do you wish?" She said to Him, "Grant that these two sons of mine may sit, one on Your right hand and the other on the left, in Your kingdom."

But Jesus answered and said, "You do not know what you ask. Are you able to drink the cup that I am about to drink, and be baptized with the baptism that I am baptized with?" They said to Him, "We are able." So He said to them, "You will indeed drink My cup, and be baptized with the baptism that I am baptized with; but to sit on My right hand and on My left is not Mine to give, but it is for those for whom it is prepared by My Father." (Mt 20:20-23)

By this reply, Jesus confirmed the high cost and sacrifice of sitting beside Him in Heaven. This requirement is summed up by participating with Christ in His pain and drinking the cup that He drank. Without a doubt St. Mary was the only one who truly participated in drinking the cup of Christ. Thus, she deserved wholeheartedly in faith, to sit on the right hand of the King in heaven.

What pain and sufferings had St. Mary passed through that Simeon the elder referenced while she was carrying her baby in the temple? Simeon said, "yes, a sword will pierce through your own soul also, that the thoughts of many hearts may be revealed." (Luke 2:35)

Since her holy pregnancy, pain and sufferings loaded on St. Mary.

1- First was the sword of doubt from St. Joseph, her fiancé, when he found that she was pregnant and wanted to leave her. That would have hurt her when she was a pure virgin. The Lord revealed the truth and her innocence to St. Joseph: "St. Joseph, son of David, do not be afraid to take to you Mary your wife, for that which is conceived in her is of the Holy Spirit" (Matt 1:20)

2- The second sword that hurt St. Mary was when she had no place to deliver her baby and was forced to give birth in a manger. The Lord though, comforted and raised her spirit through the visit of the shepherds and wiseman worshipping the baby Jesus in the manger, and offering praise and gifts. They proclaimed that Jesus will be the King, Prophet and Priest in the kingdom of God.

All these sufferings occurred as if the Lord was pronouncing to His children that in all their trials, He offers comfort and hope, just as He did with St. Mary.

3- The swords of pain and hurt continued with St. Mary when she fled to Egypt while facing all the dangers of travel. Her heart was broken when she heard about Herod killing 144,000 children in Bethlehem.

4- When St. Mary returned from Egypt to Nazareth she was faced with difficulties of the daily needs. She worked hard to support her son and husband, St. Joseph, who in turn worked as a carpenter to support his family. St. Mary always believed in the words of God that "having food and clothing, with these we shall be content." (1 Tim 6:8)

5- All the pain and tribulations in the early stages of St. Mary's life were bearable and light. However, they increased when Jesus started being known among Israel and the Pharisees. When the elders started working against Christ, and He rebuked them for their sins and hypocritical teachings, St. Mary experienced greater tribulations and pain.

St. Mary heard that Caiaphas and Herod were intending to detain Jesus to be judged before the courts. The situation then became worse after the Jewish crowd falsely claimed that Jesus of Nazareth was breaking the law and the commandments, and changing the customs and values handed down by the elders. The Jewish elders asked Pilate to put Jesus on trial and eventually brought Him in front of Pilate asking for His crucifixion. Pilate ordered the crucifixion of Christ only in fear for his powerful position, rather than finding and declaring that He committed any crime worthy of His execution. Arguably, Jesus was sentenced to be crucified out of envy and injustice, completely innocent of being convicted as a criminal and blasphemer.

ST. MARY'S FEELINGS

How sad and hurt must have St. Mary been when she saw almost all of the disciples leave Him and flee? Only John, the beloved disciple, remained until His crucifixion. St. Mary must have remembered God's prophesy to Simeon during this time to help overcome her hurt.

St. Mary was in deep mourning throughout much of Christ's ministry. Yet, bearing such mourning transformed into great comfort and joy in the end. One should learn from this that we do not surrender to the tribulations and sadness in this world but we strive to gain longsuffering like the saints who overcame the world and reaped great fruits in their hearts.

How would St. Mary have felt on the night her son was

to be crucified? Imagine St. Mary unable to sleep all night until John came to her in the morning with the unbearable news that her son, Jesus, was ordered to carry the cross and climb the Golgotha Mountain to be crucified? It's almost unimaginable. John would have asked St. Mary to accompany him to farewell Jesus. St. Mary would surely have risen up hastily and ran to the path that John told her Jesus would be crossing. When St. Mary saw her son carrying the cross, being weary of tiredness and bleeding from His organs with cuts all over His body and a crown of thorns over His head, she would have surely cried like a baby. St. Mary would have been very exhausted but still would have found energy to say to her son: "oh my son, how cruel is that sword cutting through your mum's heart seeing you like that".

Imagine St. Mary trying to come closer to Jesus to hug and farewell Him, yet was further hurt by the soldiers rebuking her and not allowing her to attempt to comfort Him. She would have followed her son from a distance saying to herself: "Where am I going? Could I go to the Golgotha Mountain? Could I stand there under my son's cross? Could I watch Him in His dying moments? Could I see Him, the one who had raised the dead and given life, be deserted by everybody?" In spite of all the hurt, St. Mary followed her son and watched His clothes being removed and led nailed to the cross in His hands and feet.

Jesus was raised on the cross while His mother was looking on. St. Mary did manage to come close to Him, with John the beloved, and even succeeded to stand under His cross. St. Mary was comforted immensely when she heard her beloved son nurturing her by saying something probably like: "why did you come here, you beloved dove? Your pain and suffering magnify my own suffering. Return to sleep until my torment subsides. There is no comfort for you here". St. Mary would have probably answered: "How can you ask me to turn my eyes away from You, my beloved Son? Your pain and suffering have drowned my heart that I cannot think of anything else. My soul is crucified and will be buried with You".

In spite of the excruciating pain that St. Mary witnessed her son suffer and her feelings of agony, one should imagine St. Mary standing courageously and confidently in front of the cross. St. Mary did not leave the crucifixion site for one moment and was confident that God, the Father, was with Him throughout the ordeal. As a loving mother she still ached from His sufferings and the fulfillment of the prophetic saying "He was led as a lamb to the slaughter, and as a sheep before its shearers is silent, so He opened not His mouth." (Isaiah

53:7), yet at the same time St. Mary was confident that her pain would change into joy in a short period of time.

When St. Mary was watching the crucifixion of Christ one could imagine her saying to Jesus: "By standing beside Your cross, my Son, and sharing in Your pain and suffering, that is an indication of my true love to You and faith in God's will to redeem mankind".

At that moment the overwhelmingly loving feelings of Jesus towards His mother clearly became evident.

JESUS WORDS AND WILL

How would Jesus, the one who had the greatest understanding of the feelings of man, have felt towards His mother after she had parented Him? How would Jesus feel after St. Mary constantly stayed awaked for her son and bore so much pain watching Him being crucified?

When Jesus saw St. Mary standing under His cross, He wanted to ease her pain. Jesus said to St. Mary: "Woman, behold your son!" Then He said to the disciple, "Behold your mother!" (Jn 19:26). Through these words we see just how great His heart is and that His love never fails.

The words of Christ to His mother implied other meanings and emotions. These included; "I am leaving this world and going to my Heavenly Father in Heaven. You do not have any siblings, husband or other children. You do not have anyone to support you in this world. Since I care so much about you, I have told John to look after you and be the beloved son in place of me, your son in the flesh. You were a loving mother for me when I was incarnated in the world. I obeyed you willingly. Now my will is to follow my Heavenly Father whose will I have now fulfilled by offering myself to redeem mankind. I am now entrusting you to the care of my beloved disciple John".

After hearing the words of Jesus to entrust John to take care of St. Mary, she would have comprehended the fact that her relationship with her son in the flesh had ended, yet she had started a new stronger spiritual relationship with Christ as her Savior and Redeemer.

If we look at St. Mary gazing her eyes upon her son and savior on the cross, through her tears we would have seen the happiness on her face that her son had fulfilled the work God had sent Him to carry out.

In spite of all the Jews, priests and soldiers mocking and

cursing Christ saying: "You who said that You will destroy the temple and build it in three days, where is Your power? Why do not You come down from the cross and save Yourself? "And: "You who save others, if you are Jesus, why do not You save Yourself?" In spite of all these rebukes and her son being crucified, St. Mary saw Him sitting with glory on His Heavenly throne crowned in victory, glory, and power.

After St. Mary experienced all these revelations from the depth of her heart based on God's words who offered a new life for all mankind, St. Mary went with John to his house. They were all waiting for the fulfillment of Christ's promise that He will be raised up in the third day.

ST. MARY IN JOHN THE BELOVED'S HOUSE

St. Mary had the nature to completely obey and follow God's commandments. After the crucifixion, St. Mary departed with John to his house while leaving the other women at the cross to see where the body of Jesus would be buried.

While Jesus was on the cross feeling His mother's agony, He wanted to alleviate her pain by sending her away from this place of sadness, suffering and pain. He would have wanted to fulfil two petitions through His command for John to look after St. Mary.

THE PETITIONS OF JESUS FOR HIS MOTHER

1- The first petition of Jesus to John was simple and intimate, and that was for John to look after His mother. He asked John, the closest to Him, to look after His mother by keeping her close. John, the beloved, acted just like a loving son; taking care of her, serving her and honoring her as she rightly deserves.

2- The second petition was more general and comprehensive. Jesus wanted to continue supporting and encouraging His disciples by providing them with divine revelations and teachings that they could hear from His mother; events and incidents that St. Mary would have experienced during the 30 years that Jesus was with her. Many things that St. Mary saw, heard, and experienced in person could strengthen the disciples and equip them with the boldness to preach the word of God to the entire world.

When St. Mary was in John's house, her comfort, happiness and condolence were that her son, Jesus, was still with her at all times. St. Mary wanted to live with Jesus and never be separated from Him. She felt His presence everywhere. We could imagine that everywhere St Mary went, she remembered His life as a man on earth; the places where He taught His disciples and became the perfect role model of dealing with suffering and fear to those who can kill the body but do not have power over the soul in Christ.

The early church writings mentioned that during St. Mary's stay in John the beloved's house, she regularly visited the holy places previously visited by Christ. On many occasions St. Mary visited the Holy place where Jesus was buried before His resurrection. The Jews were complaining and upset from this and they tried to forbid St. Mary from visiting this place because of the myriad of miracles that happened.

THE DEPARTURE OF ST. MARY

St. Mary was about 60 years old when she departed this world and all her life she lived under God's great care. God heard and answered the request of St. Mary's parents to have a child and St. Mary was born, promised to the Lord. She grew in the temple full of the Holy Spirit and deserved to be titled the second Eve, the mother of God. St. Mary raised the child Jesus, who enjoyed all the blessings during His life on earth. St. Mary witnessed the crucifixion, resurrection and ascension of Christ.

St. Mary went to John the beloved's house according to the request of the Lord. She spent her time in prayer and traveled from place to place that she previously visited with her Son. From time to time St. Mary sat with the disciples and followed up their evangelism to the entire globe. St. Mary was the spiritual anchor for the disciples, answering their questions and strengthening them.

When St. Mary witnessed how the word of God spread in Judah, Samaria and throughout the world, she longed to leave this temporal world. St. Mary was confident that salvation would be brought to the whole world. She was praying and asking her Son to take her into Heaven after she had finished her journey in this life. Her beloved Son listened to her prayer and sent His angel to inform her about the day of her departure. St. Mary was very joyful and asked her Son to allow her to see all the disciples once more before her departure. Despite all the disciples being spread out across the world, God made it miraculously possible for all of them to be present with her in John's place at the same time, except for Thomas who was in South India.

St. Mary was very joyful when she saw all of the disciples around her. She informed them of her departure and encouraged them just before her farewell from this world, as Christ brought a myriad of angels to take her pure soul in His Holy hands. The disciples surrounded her body while they were singing hymns with the invisible angels, whose prayers and glorious singing were heard loud and clear.

St. Mary's departure is celebrated on the 21st day of every Coptic month

INCIDENTS THAT ACCOMPANIED ST. MARY'S DEPARTURE

St. Mary had honored the Lord by memorising and following His word. God never forgot St. Mary's love and support of Him, and truly honored her. He did not permit any harm or evil to happen during her departure, in contrast to the excruciating pain of the death of Jesus Christ on the cross. This was very evident in two incidents:

1- The First Incident

After preparing St. Mary's body to be buried in a suitable respectful manner, the disciples carried her coffin and walked towards the tomb. The Jews then attacked the coffin and tried to stop the burial. When a mighty man called 'Theofeena' attempted to push the coffin with his hands both his hands became separated from his body and stuck to the coffin. Theofeena cried and wept with a loud voice, and was sorrowful for his deed. All those who were attacking the coffin begged the disciples for forgiveness and were very sorrowful. After Peter asked all these attackers to come closer to the coffin and touch their eyes with the clothes that were in the coffin, they were all healed, including Theofeena.

2- The second Incident

Before the disciples buried St. Mary, a group of Jews and priests sent strong soldiers to arrest and harm all the disciples while they were gathering around the coffin of St. Mary. They even surrounded John, the beloved's, house and lit fire around the house to kill everyone. However, the Lord sent a strong wind that reversed the direction of the fire that saved John's house and everyone inside, and in fact burnt those who lit the fire. The leader of the soldiers who ordered the fire to be lit, miraculously believed and was blessed by St. Mary's body. He asked the disciples to pray for him and many people believed in Christ from that day.

The disciples then buried St. Mary in Jerusalem. When the disciples continued to hear the sound of the angels singing hymns, they stayed next to the tomb. They continued praying from time to time in front of her burial place until the 16th day of the month of Mesra.

THE ASCENSION OF ST. MARY'S BODY

The body that carried the incarnated God could never be harmed by any human being, nor could it be harmed by the devil who tried to continually raise the Jews against St. Mary. The body of St. Mary, blessed by the Holy Spirit to carry God's Word, could never be encased by the dirt or sand of the earth.

If the Lord, to Him be the glory, had honored those who followed Him like Enoch and Elijah the prophet, by taking them to a special place not to be buried underground, would He not honor His mother by raising her body to paradise? Truly the honored and blessed are waiting, like St. Mary, to be confirmed in the truth that their body will ascend into heaven in a glorified body; the body that will never see corruption since she was blessed by the Holy Spirit and carried the incarnate God.

The Lord wanted all the disciples to know how much He honored his mother and strengthen their faith and hope in the eternal life. God permitted that Thomas the disciple would not be present for St. Mary's burial as He was in India at the time. The Lord allowed Thomas to see a myriad of angels carry the body of St. Mary to heaven. When Thomas enquired about the incident, the angels told him that they were carrying St. Mary's blessed body to paradise. Thomas was joyfully kneeling and kissing her body. A cloud then delivered Thomas to where the rest of the disciples were gathering around the tomb, praying and singing hymns.

After departing from the disciples, Thomas asked to see St. Mary's body for one last time. When the disciples moved the stone in front of the tomb, they did not find the body of St. Mary. Thomas comforted them all and told them what he previously witnessed. The disciples were joyful and earnestly prayed for the Lord to show them where the body was taken. The Lord listened to their prayers by taking them in spirit to the body of St Mary in paradise on the 16th of Mesra. There the disciples understood that St. Mary the Queen is waiting for the day of resurrection and will sit on the right hand of the King. The disciples also heard a voice saying: "This is the daughter who freed her mother".

MIRACLES OF ST. MARY

FREEING OF MATTHIAS AND THE MELTING OF STEEL

After the Holy Spirit descended on the disciples, they were scattered all around the world performing evangelism. The disciple Matthias went to a city called Bartow, close to Galatia, where the people were worshipping idols. When Matthias preached the word of God to them, many believed and started to destroy the idols they previously worshipped. The enemy of God enticed the idolaters against Matthias by saying that he did not respect the gods and their teachings. The governor of the city ordered that Matthias and many of the believers be imprisoned. Matthias was not afraid and kept praying earnestly for God to save him.

St. Mary, who was in Jerusalem at that time, heard about the hardship Matthias was going through. She asked her son to lead her to where Matthias was imprisoned. St. Mary was guided by the spirit to the city of Bartow where she met an old believing lady, who led her to where Mattias was imprisoned. When St. Mary came to the prison and found that all the doors were locked with steel chains, she prayed for the Lord to melt the steel. The Lord answered her prayer and all the steel in the prison and even the city melted into liquid.

All the prisoners escaped and were free. The guards rushed to tell the governor what had happened and after knowing that the prisoners escaped, he was greatly troubled and in disbelief. The governor ordered that all the prisoners be recaptured and sentenced to death. The guards informed him that they no longer had any swords or weapons because all the steel had melted. There was a big uproar in the city as all the metal doors, locks and machinery had melted.

When the governor investigated the cause of the melting, he was told about a foreign woman who asked about Matthias and prayed, powerfully, in front of the prison while suddenly all the steel melted. The governor called St. Mary and asked her how she could have melted the steel? She responded that the true God Jesus Christ was the one who melted the steel.

The son of the governor was possessed by a demon, and his father was desperate to try to heal his son from the enslavement of the devil. The governor asked that his son be brought to St. Mary, and when he saw her, he started screaming: "this is the mother of the One God". St. Mary ordered the demon to leave him immediately and subsequently left him. The young man then sat quietly and spoke normally. His father was very joyful and believed in Jesus Christ from that moment on. Many people in the city also became believers and asked St. Mary to pray for the restoration of the steel to its original nature in their city and she complied.

Most of the people in Bartow were baptized at the hands of Matthias. The governor ordered that all the idol temples be destroyed and a large church be built in the name of St. Mary. St. Mary was honored largely by the people in that city and they continually asked for her intercession.

Let us all call St. Mary during our times of tribulation. She will always hasten to save us just as she did for Matthias. May her intercession always be with us.

THE APPARITION ST. MARY

In the evening of Tuesday, the 24th Barmahat, in the year 1684 of the martyrs, the 2nd of April the year 1968 A.D., and during the reign of Pope Kyrolos the 116th Pope of Alexandria, our lady the virgin St. Mary– the pride of humanity- started to appear in holy illuminated apparitions on the top of the church domes of St. Mary's church in Zeitoun, Cairo.

These apparitions continued for several successive nights in unrivalled illumination in the east or west. The apparitions continued for hours on some nights and were seen by many people from various religions, denominations and backgrounds. All who saw her with their own eyes burst into hymns and praises towards her, accompanied with tears and prayers. St. Mary looked kindly to all those who observed her, raising her hands to bless them from all the corners of the earth.

It was in the evening when a guard at the department of Public Transport in Townan Street across the street from the church, saw an illuminated figure on top of the church dome. He called his colleagues to check what exactly was the illumination. They saw a young lady in white clothes kneeling on top of the church dome next to the cross. They were concerned for her safety because the dome was circular and had a sharp drop. They kept screaming and warning her to not fall or jump down, especially as they thought that she was attempting to commit suicide.

They called the police who arrived quickly and tried to convince the lady to immediately come down from the church dome. Strangely to all people who were watching the young beautiful lady, in shiny white clothes, she stood up and was holding an olive branch in her hands. Suddenly a flock of white doves flew from the top of her head. All present immediately recognised that they were witnessing a heavenly scene. They shone strong light beams on the lady, which only added to her brightness.

They turned off all the street lights near the church, however the light did not vanish and in fact became clearer and brighter. The lady started to circle the dome in all directions, surrounded by an aura of light. It was then that those present recognised that the lady was St. Mary. They all burst into hymns and praises in a loud voice. This continued throughout the night until the morning.

Since the first apparition of St. Mary, she continued to appear at the top of the church dome in further apparitions. She was seen by thousands of men, women and children, including Egyptian and foreigners, Christians and non-Christians. Her apparition was accompanied with the holy bodies and doves that filled the sky creating a heavenly atmosphere above this material world.

St. Mary appeared to many people between the central and Southern domes of the church in several apparitions:

• Once she was a glistering figure of a young woman in real human size and sometimes even larger

• Once her head and body were covered with a long shining silver or dark sky blue headcover

• Once her body was very thin, like phosphorus light baby blue or bright white in colour

• Once her head was looking downwards in a mournful appearance

• Once she was looking to the cross, while the cross itself was shining in spite of the fact that it was made of dark steel

The light from these apparitions of St. Mary extended

and covered most of the roof of the church. St. Mary raised and lowered her hands in some cases, while in others she would put them in front of her bosom. She always looked calm and peaceful, and was often accompanied with a tall angel behind her with outstretched wings.

Another apparition of St. Mary was a scene of her looking like a heavenly queen standing in great awesome light. Her face was surrounded by a halo of golden light colour. She had a shining crown on her head that sometimes appeared with a small cross on top of it. In other apparitions she would carry the baby Jesus on her left arm with a crown of jewels on His head. Other times she would be seen gathering her long garment with her hands, while in other apparitions she would raise her hands and appeared to bless those looking at her. St. Mary would continue to let all those present see her in order that no one would be deprived of her blessings.

Another frequent apparition of St. Mary depicted her as a young beautiful lady with a white headcover glancing from one of the openings in the Northern dome of the church. St. Mary would look out of the opening, nod her head or raise her hands to salute and bless the people.

The opening of the Northern dome was always very dark. None of the light from the church shone from the north because the church roof was under the dome. However, when St Mary appeared from the opening in the Northern dome, a small light shone on the dome. This illumination then became more apparent with baby blue sky like colour around it. Slowly the rays of light moved towards the dome from the inside, towards the upper body of St. Mary. Her head was covered in light blue colour reaching her shoulders. Her upper body would come out of the dome then into the sky above the church. Sometimes her full body appeared in the apparition and she would stand on top of the sliding dome. This apparition could last several minutes and sometimes even up to half an hour. After several minutes the stream of light would often fade before it disappeared. Other times the illumination would appear in the same way several times. This happened on the night of celebrating the entry of the Holy Family into Egypt on the 24th Bashans, the first of June 1968. On that day St. Mary appeared towards the Northern-Eastern dome of the church several times in succession. Her first apparition started at 10:00pm until the dawn of the following day, and many people witnessing her apparitions were blessed by her.

Another apparition of St. Mary occurred on the Northern-Western dome of the church. In this apparition she appeared as a clear translucent body, standing tall in a small size inside the opening of the dome. Her body was complete from head to toe but in a miniature size to fit into the dome opening. She was full of light, and her peace and tranquility were transferred unto all those who were looking at her.

St. Mary's apparition was, most of the time, accompanied with holy bright heavenly creatures that looked like doves or sometimes even larger creatures in size than doves. These creatures appeared passed midnight until 3:00 am in the morning. It is well known that doves do not fly at night which proves that these creatures were supernatural. These creatures were especially bright at their top and bottom end. They appeared from the midst of darkness and flew with outstretched wings without any fluttering. They flew very quickly from one side of the sky to the other. No-one was able to determine where exactly the creatures came from and how they suddenly disappeared when light appeared in the sky. Sometimes they appeared as if they were coming from inside the biggest dome, flying towards the Northern-Eastern dome, where they disappeared but quickly re-appeared a few seconds later in the other direction.

These heavenly creatures in the form of doves appeared in different ways. In some apparitions only one dove appeared, or in pairs, while in other apparitions three of them would appear like a triangle. At other times, the doves appeared in seven, ten or twelve in number, where they either made a shape of the cross while they were flying or at other times flew in parallel.

Among the spiritual signs accompanying the apparition of St. Mary was the appearance of stars in unusual sizes falling very quickly on the middle dome of the church. The stars then disappeared while they were very bright. In some apparitions, the stars appeared the size of a ball, shining very brightly when falling. At other times the stars would take the shape of a bright lantern of average size.

Included among the regular sightings of the apparitions of the Virgin St. Mary was the apparition of an orange light that spread over the Northern-Eastern dome of the church from all directions. After a few minutes from its appearance, the light would move towards the large dome and engulf it from all sides.

In many other cases of the apparitions of St. Mary the bright white light appeared to have come from inside the Northern-Eastern dome with shades of blue, similar to the sky during sunrise. The light appeared in the midst of the dome and spread to the top, almost as if the light was hung on the top part of the dome. At other times the light appeared in the midst of the dome in a white circular or oval shape. The light moved slowly towards the outside through one of the dome openings or windows, which then changed into St

Mary's upper body.

Another form of the apparition was great light in the shape of a cross with equal sides, shining brightly and magnificently on the Southern-Western dome, the Northern-Eastern dome or the middle dome.

Further apparitions including the middle dome being flooded with white incense that spread on the roof of the church and rose up in the sky 30 or 40m. The incense that spread on top of the dome and the church roof, was very dense and could not have been generated by thousands of incense offerings. If the incense was not so white and fragrant, one would have thought the source came from a huge fire. There were also bright cloud formations that suddenly appeared around the church. The cloud sometimes gradually changed into the shape of St. Mary. In other apparitions, St. Mary would suddenly appear from the clouds like a neon light would suddenly appear when it is switched on.

All these scenes and apparitions of St. Mary on top of the church in El Zeitoun point to a number of prophecies and indications of great somber events. Perhaps these heavenly revelations were assurances that God would always look after the church, His people and nation. His care and love are always treasured by believers and they are proud to be called Christians. In humility one should repent from their sins and come back to God. By these great signs from heaven, we may have entered the last days of this temporal world. This may well be the beginning of the end.

May God's mercy be upon us and look after His people and church, and destroy the power of evil through the intercession of the Holy Virgin, full of glory, our Lady and pride of humanity St. Mary. Amen

www.ingramcontent.com/pod-product-compliance
Lightning Source LLC
Chambersburg PA
CBHW051849040426
42447CB00006B/775